EP Math 4
Printables

This book belongs to

_____

This book was made for your convenience. It is available for printing from the Easy Peasy All-in-One Homeschool website. It contains all of the printables from Easy Peasy's Math 4 course. The instructions for each page are found in the online course.

Easy Peasy All-in-One Homeschool is a free online homeschool curriculum providing high quality education for children around the globe. It provides complete courses for pre-school through high school graduation. For EP's curriculum visit allinonehomeschool.com.

ISBN-13: 978-1548869380
ISBN-10: 1548869384

Contents

Contents

Date _____

Telling Time & Adding 2-Digits

A. Draw the hands on each clock face to show the time.

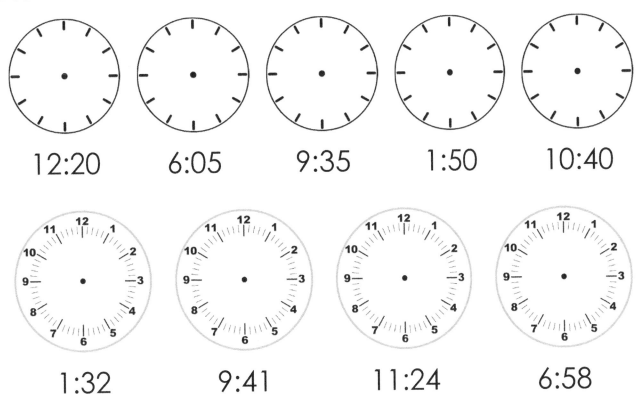

12:20   6:05   9:35   1:50   10:40

1:32   9:41   11:24   6:58

B. Solve the addition problems. The first one is done for you!

1					
59	23	74	68	49	20
+ 83	+ 74	+ 52	+ 34	+ 75	+ 35
142					

17	54	74	37	28	58
+ 92	+ 58	+ 94	+ 86	+ 68	+ 42

Date _____

Fractions & Subtracting 2-Digits

A. Write the fraction that represents the shaded parts of each group.

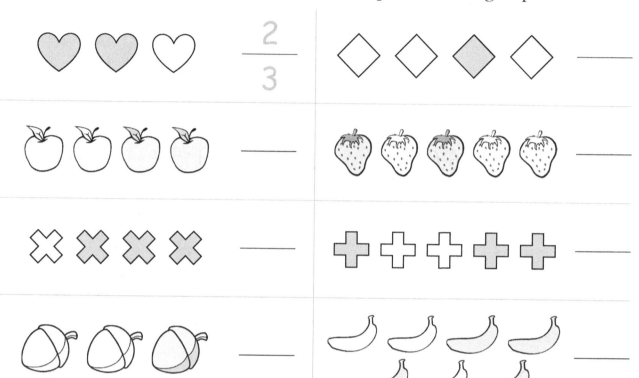

B. Solve the subtraction problems. The first one is done for you!

$$\begin{array}{r} {\scriptstyle 6\ 14} \\ \cancel{7}\cancel{4} \\ -\ 5\ 8 \\ \hline 1\ 6 \end{array}$$
$$\begin{array}{r} 72 \\ -\ 27 \\ \hline \end{array}$$
$$\begin{array}{r} 75 \\ -\ 45 \\ \hline \end{array}$$
$$\begin{array}{r} 63 \\ -\ 49 \\ \hline \end{array}$$
$$\begin{array}{r} 29 \\ -\ 25 \\ \hline \end{array}$$
$$\begin{array}{r} 83 \\ -\ 67 \\ \hline \end{array}$$

$$\begin{array}{r} 84 \\ -\ 29 \\ \hline \end{array}$$
$$\begin{array}{r} 96 \\ -\ 56 \\ \hline \end{array}$$
$$\begin{array}{r} 60 \\ -\ 18 \\ \hline \end{array}$$
$$\begin{array}{r} 95 \\ -\ 63 \\ \hline \end{array}$$
$$\begin{array}{r} 67 \\ -\ 30 \\ \hline \end{array}$$
$$\begin{array}{r} 91 \\ -\ 58 \\ \hline \end{array}$$

Adding and Subtracting Money

Add or subtract money. Don't forget the currency symbol and decimal point.

$$\begin{array}{r} \$2.00 \\ + \ \$3.47 \\ \hline \end{array} \qquad \begin{array}{r} \$5.54 \\ + \ \$0.32 \\ \hline \end{array} \qquad \begin{array}{r} \$8.02 \\ + \ \$0.16 \\ \hline \end{array} \qquad \begin{array}{r} \$4.65 \\ + \ \$3.02 \\ \hline \end{array}$$

$$\begin{array}{r} \$4.13 \\ + \ \$4.76 \\ \hline \end{array} \qquad \begin{array}{r} \$3.45 \\ + \ \$3.24 \\ \hline \end{array} \qquad \begin{array}{r} \$2.46 \\ + \ \$6.23 \\ \hline \end{array} \qquad \begin{array}{r} \$4.02 \\ + \ \$5.57 \\ \hline \end{array}$$

$$\begin{array}{r} \$6.72 \\ + \ \$2.15 \\ \hline \end{array} \qquad \begin{array}{r} \$3.42 \\ + \ \$5.36 \\ \hline \end{array} \qquad \begin{array}{r} \$2.49 \\ - \ \$0.32 \\ \hline \end{array} \qquad \begin{array}{r} \$7.94 \\ - \ \$4.52 \\ \hline \end{array}$$

$$\begin{array}{r} \$8.56 \\ - \ \$0.36 \\ \hline \end{array} \qquad \begin{array}{r} \$6.48 \\ - \ \$3.05 \\ \hline \end{array} \qquad \begin{array}{r} \$2.96 \\ - \ \$1.43 \\ \hline \end{array} \qquad \begin{array}{r} \$4.58 \\ - \ \$0.26 \\ \hline \end{array}$$

Pound $\qquad$ Euro $\qquad$ Chinese Yuan $\qquad$ Russian Ruble

$$\begin{array}{r} £9.58 \\ - \ £3.14 \\ \hline \end{array} \qquad \begin{array}{r} €8.64 \\ - \ €3.42 \\ \hline \end{array} \qquad \begin{array}{r} ¥9.47 \\ - \ ¥2.17 \\ \hline \end{array} \qquad \begin{array}{r} ₽7.63 \\ - \ ₽2.20 \\ \hline \end{array}$$

Date _____

Estimating Sums & Adding 3-Digits

Estimate the sums by rounding the numbers to the nearest hundred. Solve the actual problems for the first four as well.

$$378 \rightarrow$$
$$+ 239 \rightarrow +$$
_____

$$981 \rightarrow$$
$$+ 863 \rightarrow +$$
_____

$$453 \rightarrow$$
$$+ 897 \rightarrow +$$
_____

$$728 \rightarrow$$
$$+ 683 \rightarrow +$$
_____

$$638 \rightarrow$$
$$+ 550 \rightarrow +$$
estimate:

$$207 \rightarrow$$
$$+ 554 \rightarrow +$$
estimate:

$$891 \rightarrow$$
$$+ 626 \rightarrow +$$
estimate:

$$432 \rightarrow$$
$$+ 237 \rightarrow +$$
estimate:

$$853 \rightarrow$$
$$+ 728 \rightarrow +$$
estimate:

$$950 \rightarrow$$
$$+ 394 \rightarrow +$$
estimate:

Estimating Differences & Subtracting 3-Digits

Estimate the differences by rounding the numbers to the nearest hundred. Solve the actual problems for the first four as well.

$$928 \rightarrow$$
$$- 529 \rightarrow -$$
_____

$$647 \rightarrow$$
$$- 290 \rightarrow -$$
_____

$$896 \rightarrow$$
$$- 134 \rightarrow -$$
_____

$$827 \rightarrow$$
$$- 562 \rightarrow -$$
_____

$$761 \rightarrow$$
$$- 438 \rightarrow -$$
_____

estimate:

$$743 \rightarrow$$
$$- 286 \rightarrow -$$
_____

estimate:

$$441 \rightarrow$$
$$- 373 \rightarrow -$$
_____

estimate:

$$835 \rightarrow$$
$$- 329 \rightarrow -$$
_____

estimate:

$$750 \rightarrow$$
$$- 195 \rightarrow -$$
_____

estimate:

$$881 \rightarrow$$
$$- 207 \rightarrow -$$
_____

estimate:

Date _____

Estimating Sums & Adding 4-Digits

A. Estimate the sums by rounding the numbers to the nearest hundred.

$$8584 \rightarrow $$
$$+\ 3205 \rightarrow +\ \underline{}$$

$$9228 \rightarrow $$
$$+\ 6150 \rightarrow +\ \underline{}$$

$$3928 \rightarrow $$
$$+\ 6249 \rightarrow +\ \underline{}$$

$$7868 \rightarrow $$
$$+\ 4762 \rightarrow +\ \underline{}$$

B. Estimate the sums by rounding the numbers to the nearest thousand.

$$4352 \rightarrow $$
$$+\ 6787 \rightarrow +\ \underline{}$$

$$8334 \rightarrow $$
$$+\ 5607 \rightarrow +\ \underline{}$$

$$2983 \rightarrow $$
$$+\ 6065 \rightarrow +\ \underline{}$$

$$7500 \rightarrow $$
$$+\ 7456 \rightarrow +\ \underline{}$$

C. Choose four problems above to find the exact sums. You can solve all eight problems if you want!

Estimating Differences & Subtracting 4-Digits

A. Estimate the differences by rounding the numbers to the nearest hundred.

$$4665 \rightarrow$$
$$-\ 1258 \rightarrow\ -\ _____$$

$$8578 \rightarrow$$
$$-\ 4937 \rightarrow\ -\ _____$$

$$5930 \rightarrow$$
$$-\ 1675 \rightarrow\ -\ _____$$

$$7278 \rightarrow$$
$$-\ 3693 \rightarrow\ -\ _____$$

B. Estimate the differences by rounding the numbers to the nearest thousand.

$$8362 \rightarrow$$
$$-\ 5756 \rightarrow\ -\ _____$$

$$7432 \rightarrow$$
$$-\ 5867 \rightarrow\ -\ _____$$

$$9116 \rightarrow$$
$$-\ 6569 \rightarrow\ -\ _____$$

$$5819 \rightarrow$$
$$-\ 2982 \rightarrow\ -\ _____$$

C. Choose four problems above to find the exact differences. You can solve all eight problems if you want!

Date _____

Place Value and Expanded Notation

A. How many hundreds, tens, and ones are in the number **405**?

405 = [ ] hundreds + [ ] tens + [ ] ones

B. Write the number **405** in expanded form, or expanded notation.

405 = [ ] + [ ]

C. Write each number in standard form.

70 + 6 = _____   800 + 20 + 9 = _____

500 + 4 = _____   2,000 + 70 + 1 = _____

200 + 50 = _____   3,000 + 100 + 7 = _____

900 + 40 = _____   8,000 + 200 + 90 + 5 = _____

D. Write each number in expanded form.

82 = _____

463 = _____

305 = _____

350 = _____

5,281 = _____

Place Value to Thousands

A. Cut out the number cards below. Read each number out loud. Put two boxes together with the biggest number first and then read what that number would be. Have someone who knows their big numbers check you.

B. Write seven of the numbers in the first column of the table in Lesson 15.

CUT ALONG DOTTED LINES

886	64
653	2,547
3,705	110
422	8,021
5,819	238

This page is left blank for the cutting activity
on the opposite side.

Date _____

Place Value to Thousands

Pick seven numbers from the number cards in Lesson 14 and write them in the **Standard** column. Write each number in expanded and word form.

Standard	Expanded	Word

Date _____

Place Value Houses

Write a digit other than zero in each room in each house. Read your number.
Have someone who knows their big numbers check you.

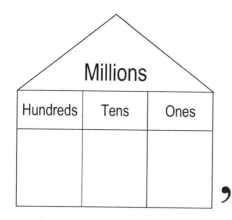

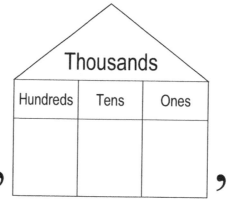

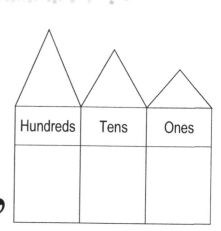

Place Value to Millions

Cut out the number cards at the bottom of the page. Put them together to make big numbers. Say each number you make. Write down two of the numbers in standard, expanded, and word form.

Standard:

Expanded:

Word:

Standard:

Expanded:

Word:

CUT ALONG DOTTED LINES

| 1 | 2 | 3 | 4 | 5 | , |
| 6 | 7 | 8 | 9 | 0 | , |

This page is left blank for the cutting activity
on the opposite side.

Place Value to Millions

Write the value of each underlined digit in words.

ones   *tens*   ten thousands   **thousands**

hundreds   hundred thousands   millions

47,531   thousands _____

2,429 _____

19,270 _____

25,286 _____

63,744 _____

142,625 _____

731,823 _____

423,212 _____

2,254,065 _____

8,564,159 _____

4,378,387 _____

Date _____

Place Value to Millions

A. Write each number in expanded form.

32,917 =

_____

54,890 =

_____

672,039 =

_____

_____

2,803,426 =

_____

_____

4,367,204 =

_____

_____

B. Write 4-digit numbers. Then write each number in expanded form.

_____ = _____

_____ = _____

C. Write 5-digit numbers. Then write each number in expanded form.

_____ = _____

_____ = _____

Date _____

Place Value to Millions

A. Write each number in standard or expanded form to complete the table.

	7,000 + 300 + 20 + 5
406,932	
9,312,507	

B. Write each number in standard or word form to complete the table.

12,368	
	two hundred forty-two thousand, seven hundred nineteen
4,502,587	

Date _____

Mental Math Strategies

A. Add or subtract mentally. Use expanded notation or rounding.

58 + 66 = _____   85 − 43 = _____

372 + 798 = _____   525 − 456 = _____

852 + 247 = _____   787 + 434 = _____

B. Solve each word problem mentally.

Ron collects stamps. He collected 58 flower stamps and 46 bird stamps. How many stamps did Ron collect all together?

Roger has 966 red marbles and 759 blue marbles. Mark has 834 red marbles and 763 blue marbles. Who has more marbles?

_____   _____

Grace had 987 smiley stickers. She gave 879 of them to her sister Angela. How many stickers does Grace have now?

Mia needs to solve 35 problems. She has solved 18 problems so far. How many problems does Mia still need to solve?

_____   _____

Sam read 176 pages of his reading assignment last week. He read 189 pages this week. How many pages did Sam read in all?

The candy store sold 453 candies last week. It sold 328 candies this week. How many candies did the candy store sell in total?

_____   _____

Multiplying 2-Digits

Let's practice multiplying bigger numbers. The first two are done for you!

| $\begin{array}{r} {}^{2} \\ 16 \\ \times\ 4 \\ \hline 64 \end{array}$ | $\begin{array}{r} {}^{3} \\ 98 \\ \times\ 4 \\ \hline 392 \end{array}$ | $\begin{array}{r} 41 \\ \times\ 3 \\ \hline \end{array}$ | $\begin{array}{r} 41 \\ \times\ 30 \\ \hline \end{array}$ | $\begin{array}{r} 27 \\ \times\ 5 \\ \hline \end{array}$ |

| $\begin{array}{r} 81 \\ \times\ 6 \\ \hline \end{array}$ | $\begin{array}{r} 27 \\ \times\ 3 \\ \hline \end{array}$ | $\begin{array}{r} 39 \\ \times\ 2 \\ \hline \end{array}$ | $\begin{array}{r} 68 \\ \times\ 5 \\ \hline \end{array}$ | $\begin{array}{r} 50 \\ \times\ 4 \\ \hline \end{array}$ |

| $\begin{array}{r} 52 \\ \times\ 4 \\ \hline \end{array}$ | $\begin{array}{r} 36 \\ \times\ 7 \\ \hline \end{array}$ | $\begin{array}{r} 96 \\ \times\ 8 \\ \hline \end{array}$ | $\begin{array}{r} 23 \\ \times\ 2 \\ \hline \end{array}$ | $\begin{array}{r} 34 \\ \times\ 9 \\ \hline \end{array}$ |

Date _____

Multiplying 2-Digits

Solve the multiplication problems.

$$\begin{array}{r} 75 \\ \times\ 57 \\ \hline \end{array} \qquad \begin{array}{r} 35 \\ \times\ 49 \\ \hline \end{array} \qquad \begin{array}{r} 42 \\ \times\ 68 \\ \hline \end{array} \qquad \begin{array}{r} 79 \\ \times\ 60 \\ \hline \end{array} \qquad \begin{array}{r} 95 \\ \times\ 84 \\ \hline \end{array}$$

$$\begin{array}{r} 52 \\ \times\ 26 \\ \hline \end{array} \qquad \begin{array}{r} 88 \\ \times\ 37 \\ \hline \end{array} \qquad \begin{array}{r} 39 \\ \times\ 46 \\ \hline \end{array} \qquad \begin{array}{r} 63 \\ \times\ 35 \\ \hline \end{array} \qquad \begin{array}{r} 80 \\ \times\ 43 \\ \hline \end{array}$$

$$\begin{array}{r} 10 \\ \times\ 72 \\ \hline \end{array} \qquad \begin{array}{r} 48 \\ \times\ 53 \\ \hline \end{array} \qquad \begin{array}{r} 26 \\ \times\ 65 \\ \hline \end{array} \qquad \begin{array}{r} 29 \\ \times\ 75 \\ \hline \end{array} \qquad \begin{array}{r} 86 \\ \times\ 23 \\ \hline \end{array}$$

Date _____

Multiplying 2-Digits

Solve the multiplication problems.

$$
\begin{array}{r} 43 \\ \times\ 86 \\ \hline \end{array}
\qquad
\begin{array}{r} 90 \\ \times\ 57 \\ \hline \end{array}
\qquad
\begin{array}{r} 75 \\ \times\ 36 \\ \hline \end{array}
\qquad
\begin{array}{r} 25 \\ \times\ 73 \\ \hline \end{array}
\qquad
\begin{array}{r} 63 \\ \times\ 48 \\ \hline \end{array}
$$

$$
\begin{array}{r} 28 \\ \times\ 65 \\ \hline \end{array}
\qquad
\begin{array}{r} 56 \\ \times\ 47 \\ \hline \end{array}
\qquad
\begin{array}{r} 19 \\ \times\ 82 \\ \hline \end{array}
\qquad
\begin{array}{r} 93 \\ \times\ 68 \\ \hline \end{array}
\qquad
\begin{array}{r} 79 \\ \times\ 30 \\ \hline \end{array}
$$

$$
\begin{array}{r} 85 \\ \times\ 17 \\ \hline \end{array}
\qquad
\begin{array}{r} 50 \\ \times\ 72 \\ \hline \end{array}
\qquad
\begin{array}{r} 43 \\ \times\ 86 \\ \hline \end{array}
\qquad
\begin{array}{r} 92 \\ \times\ 55 \\ \hline \end{array}
\qquad
\begin{array}{r} 64 \\ \times\ 29 \\ \hline \end{array}
$$

Date _____

Multiplying 3-Digits

Solve the multiplication problems. Two problems are done for you!

$$
\begin{array}{r}
875 \\
\times \quad 6 \\
\hline
5{,}250
\end{array}
\qquad
\begin{array}{r}
616 \\
\times \quad 4 \\
\hline
\end{array}
\qquad
\begin{array}{r}
411 \\
\times \quad 56 \\
\hline
2{,}466 \\
+\ 20{,}550 \\
\hline
23{,}016
\end{array}
\qquad
\begin{array}{r}
251 \\
\times \quad 98 \\
\hline
\end{array}
$$

$$
\begin{array}{r}
746 \\
\times \quad 58 \\
\hline
\end{array}
\qquad
\begin{array}{r}
362 \\
\times \quad 68 \\
\hline
\end{array}
\qquad
\begin{array}{r}
147 \\
\times \quad 95 \\
\hline
\end{array}
\qquad
\begin{array}{r}
950 \\
\times \quad 27 \\
\hline
\end{array}
$$

$$
\begin{array}{r}
906 \\
\times \quad 43 \\
\hline
\end{array}
\qquad
\begin{array}{r}
578 \\
\times \quad 34 \\
\hline
\end{array}
\qquad
\begin{array}{r}
482 \\
\times \quad 91 \\
\hline
\end{array}
\qquad
\begin{array}{r}
326 \\
\times \quad 27 \\
\hline
\end{array}
$$

Date _____

Multiplying 3-Digits

Solve the multiplication problems.

$$720 \times 532$$ $$495 \times 253$$ $$787 \times 321$$ $$538 \times 694$$

$$578 \times 975$$ $$810 \times 641$$ $$452 \times 930$$ $$293 \times 382$$

Date _____

Multiplying 3-Digits

Solve the multiplication problems.

$$
\begin{array}{r} 201 \\ \times \quad 374 \\ \hline \end{array}
\qquad
\begin{array}{r} 392 \\ \times \quad 549 \\ \hline \end{array}
\qquad
\begin{array}{r} 800 \\ \times \quad 270 \\ \hline \end{array}
\qquad
\begin{array}{r} 476 \\ \times \quad 305 \\ \hline \end{array}
$$

$$
\begin{array}{r} 391 \\ \times \quad 367 \\ \hline \end{array}
\qquad
\begin{array}{r} 125 \\ \times \quad 746 \\ \hline \end{array}
\qquad
\begin{array}{r} 820 \\ \times \quad 342 \\ \hline \end{array}
\qquad
\begin{array}{r} 564 \\ \times \quad 486 \\ \hline \end{array}
$$

Multiplying 2-Digits

Solve the multiplication problems.

$$
\begin{array}{r} 31 \\ \times\ 7 \\ \hline \end{array}
\qquad
\begin{array}{r} 46 \\ \times\ 8 \\ \hline \end{array}
\qquad
\begin{array}{r} 34 \\ \times\ 9 \\ \hline \end{array}
\qquad
\begin{array}{r} 57 \\ \times\ 5 \\ \hline \end{array}
\qquad
\begin{array}{r} 48 \\ \times\ 0 \\ \hline \end{array}
$$

$$
\begin{array}{r} 50 \\ \times\ 8 \\ \hline \end{array}
\qquad
\begin{array}{r} 84 \\ \times\ 2 \\ \hline \end{array}
\qquad
\begin{array}{r} 17 \\ \times\ 1 \\ \hline \end{array}
\qquad
\begin{array}{r} 95 \\ \times\ 6 \\ \hline \end{array}
\qquad
\begin{array}{r} 63 \\ \times\ 7 \\ \hline \end{array}
$$

$$
\begin{array}{r} 61 \\ \times\ 9 \\ \hline \end{array}
\qquad
\begin{array}{r} 39 \\ \times\ 7 \\ \hline \end{array}
\qquad
\begin{array}{r} 58 \\ \times\ 3 \\ \hline \end{array}
\qquad
\begin{array}{r} 82 \\ \times\ 4 \\ \hline \end{array}
\qquad
\begin{array}{r} 71 \\ \times\ 3 \\ \hline \end{array}
$$

Date _____

Multiplying 2-Digits

Solve the multiplication problems.

```
    20          15          54          63          23
  × 42        × 38        × 41        × 25        × 94
  _____      _____      _____      _____      _____


    34          95          48          21          86
  × 22        × 85        × 73        × 60        × 36
  _____      _____      _____      _____      _____


    50          16          62          39          87
  × 92        × 73        × 49        × 52        × 29
  _____      _____      _____      _____      _____
```

Date _____

Multiplying 3-Digits

Solve the multiplication problems.

```
      511          830          489          574
   ×   73       ×   19       ×   65       ×   61
```

```
      604          427          509          781
   ×   28       ×   67       ×   52       ×   90
```

```
      895          248          758          677
   ×   81       ×   43       ×   66       ×   29
```

Date _____

Multiplying 3-Digits

Solve the multiplication problems.

$$
\begin{array}{r} 908 \\ \times \ 122 \\ \hline \end{array}
\qquad
\begin{array}{r} 786 \\ \times \ 195 \\ \hline \end{array}
\qquad
\begin{array}{r} 357 \\ \times \ 774 \\ \hline \end{array}
\qquad
\begin{array}{r} 569 \\ \times \ 665 \\ \hline \end{array}
$$

$$
\begin{array}{r} 914 \\ \times \ 558 \\ \hline \end{array}
\qquad
\begin{array}{r} 306 \\ \times \ 392 \\ \hline \end{array}
\qquad
\begin{array}{r} 832 \\ \times \ 747 \\ \hline \end{array}
\qquad
\begin{array}{r} 138 \\ \times \ 376 \\ \hline \end{array}
$$

$$
\begin{array}{r} 316 \\ \times \ 806 \\ \hline \end{array}
\qquad
\begin{array}{r} 643 \\ \times \ 311 \\ \hline \end{array}
\qquad
\begin{array}{r} 419 \\ \times \ 570 \\ \hline \end{array}
\qquad
\begin{array}{r} 845 \\ \times \ 432 \\ \hline \end{array}
$$

Estimating Products

A. Estimate each product by rounding the top number to the nearest hundred and the bottom number to the nearest ten and then multiplying the first digits.

$$
\begin{array}{r}
458 \rightarrow \\
\times \quad 34 \rightarrow
\end{array}
\quad \times \underline{\qquad}
$$

estimate:

$$
\begin{array}{r}
325 \rightarrow \\
\times \quad 49 \rightarrow
\end{array}
\quad \times \underline{\qquad}
$$

estimate:

$$
\begin{array}{r}
913 \rightarrow \\
\times \quad 54 \rightarrow
\end{array}
\quad \times \underline{\qquad}
$$

estimate:

$$
\begin{array}{r}
769 \rightarrow \\
\times \quad 86 \rightarrow
\end{array}
\quad \times \underline{\qquad}
$$

estimate:

$$
\begin{array}{r}
521 \rightarrow \\
\times \quad 87 \rightarrow
\end{array}
\quad \times \underline{\qquad}
$$

estimate:

$$
\begin{array}{r}
850 \rightarrow \\
\times \quad 93 \rightarrow
\end{array}
\quad \times \underline{\qquad}
$$

estimate:

$$
\begin{array}{r}
926 \rightarrow \\
\times \quad 11 \rightarrow
\end{array}
\quad \times \underline{\qquad}
$$

estimate:

$$
\begin{array}{r}
392 \rightarrow \\
\times \quad 35 \rightarrow
\end{array}
\quad \times \underline{\qquad}
$$

estimate:

B. Estimate the product by rounding the first number to the nearest thousand and the second number to the nearest hundred.

$$5{,}678 \times 504 = \boxed{} \times \boxed{} = \boxed{}$$

Date _____

Estimating Products

A. Estimate each product by rounding the top number to the nearest hundred and the bottom number to the nearest ten and then multiplying the first digits. Solve the actual problems as well.

$$433 \rightarrow$$
$$\times \quad 38 \rightarrow \quad \times \underline{\hspace{3cm}}$$

$$321 \rightarrow$$
$$\times \quad 14 \rightarrow \quad \times \underline{\hspace{3cm}}$$

$$797 \rightarrow$$
$$\times \quad 53 \rightarrow \quad \times \underline{\hspace{3cm}}$$

$$704 \rightarrow$$
$$\times \quad 62 \rightarrow \quad \times \underline{\hspace{3cm}}$$

B. Find the difference between the actual and the estimated answers.

$$- \underline{\hspace{2cm}} \qquad - \underline{\hspace{2cm}} \qquad - \underline{\hspace{2cm}} \qquad - \underline{\hspace{2cm}}$$

Lesson 54

Lesson 54   Date _____

Fraction Word Problems

For each word problem, make a labeled sketch and write an equation. Explain your answer to someone. The first one is done for you!

After school, Adam spent $\frac{1}{4}$ of an hour on math, $\frac{1}{4}$ on reading, and $\frac{1}{4}$ on science. What fraction of an hour did he spend on studying?

Labeled Sketch:

$^1/_4$	$^1/_4$	$^1/_4$
math	reading	science

Equation:

$$\frac{1}{4} + \frac{1}{4} + \frac{1}{4} = \frac{3}{4} \text{ hour}$$

Kyle had $\frac{5}{6}$ of a carton of eggs. After he used some to bake cookies, $\frac{1}{6}$ of the carton was left. What fraction of the carton did Kyle use?

Labeled Sketch: Equation:

The morning break lasts $\frac{5}{8}$ of an hour. Danny spent $\frac{2}{8}$ of an hour jumping rope. What fraction of an hour did he have left after that?

Labeled Sketch: Equation:

EP Math 4 Printables · 35

Date _____

Fraction Word Problems

For each word problem, make a labeled sketch and write an equation. Explain your answer to someone.

The store had $\frac{5}{6}$ of a box of apples. It sold $\frac{3}{6}$ of the box in the morning. What fraction of the box did the store have left after that?

Labeled Sketch: Equation:

Walter bought three boxes of fruit. They weigh $1\frac{2}{6}$ pounds, $1\frac{2}{6}$ pounds, and $2\frac{1}{6}$ pounds. What is the total weight of the three boxes?

Labeled Sketch: Equation:

Tracy used $1\frac{2}{8}$ gallons of red paint, $2\frac{1}{8}$ gallons of blue paint, and $2\frac{3}{8}$ gallons of white paint to paint her house. How many gallons of paint did Tracy use in total?

Labeled Sketch: Equation:

Fraction Word Problems

For each word problem, make a labeled sketch and write an equation. Explain your answer to someone. The first one is done for you!

The city has a beautiful 2 mile trail. Claire walked the first $1\frac{1}{4}$ miles of the trail and ran the rest. How far did she run?

Labeled Sketch: Equation:

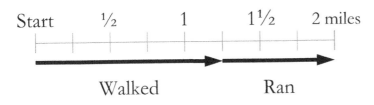

$$2 - 1\frac{1}{4} = \frac{3}{4} \text{ mile}$$

Matt went for a walk on the trail. He walked $\frac{3}{4}$ of a mile. Then he turned around and walked back to the start of the trail. How many miles did he walk in all?

Labeled Sketch: Equation:

Jacob decided to run the whole trail. After running $1\frac{3}{8}$ miles, he got tired and decided to walk the rest. How far did he have to walk to finish the trail?

Labeled Sketch: Equation:

Start   ½   1   1½   2 miles

Date _____

Fraction Word Problems

For each word problem, make a labeled sketch and write an equation. Explain your answer to someone. The track is 2 miles long.

Chris went for a walk on the trail. He walked $1\frac{1}{8}$ of a mile. Then he turned around and walked back to the start. How many miles did he walk in all?

Labeled Sketch: Equation:

Laura ran to the $\frac{3}{4}$ mile marker and ran back to the $\frac{1}{4}$ mile marker. Then she turned around and ran the rest of the trail. How many miles did she run in all?

Labeled Sketch: Equation:

Everyday Justin walks the trail. When he gets to the $1\frac{1}{4}$ mile marker, he turns around and walks back to the start. How many miles does he walk in 5 days?

Labeled Sketch: Equation:

Date _____

Long Division Lapbook

For Lessons 61 through 65, cut out the pieces as instructed to make a long division lapbook.

Division Terms

Cut this out as one piece (recommended) or divide it up into three pieces and draw the dividing line yourself. Fold each of the blank sides over the words so that the words are hidden. Write a division problem on the covers. You could write 75 for the dividend, 5 for the divisor, and 15 for the quotient. Or use your own problem.

Quotient

Divisor

Dividend

Long Division Steps

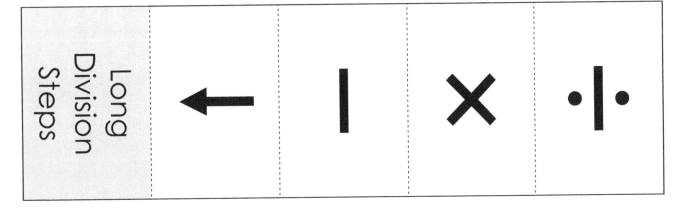

This page is left blank for the cutting activity
on the opposite side.

Individual Steps

Step 2

Step 3

Then what?

Step 4

This page is left blank for the cutting activity
on the opposite side.

Check Answer

How Do You Check
Your Answer?

First Thing

Write inside:
The first thing I need to do is …
(you write the rest).

Number Pocket

Cut out along the solid lines and fold along the dotted lines. Fold the back section up and then glue down the flaps to form a pocket. Attach to your lapbook.

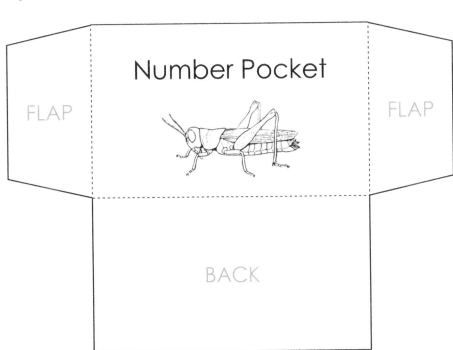

Number Pocket

FLAP

FLAP

BACK

This page is left blank for the cutting activity
on the opposite side.

Numbers

Cut out the numbers along the solid lines. Fold each number in half along the dotted line. Store the numbers in the number pocket.

Below are the numbers that will make up your practice problems. The 84 is your Dividend. The 3, 4 and 6 are your Divisors.

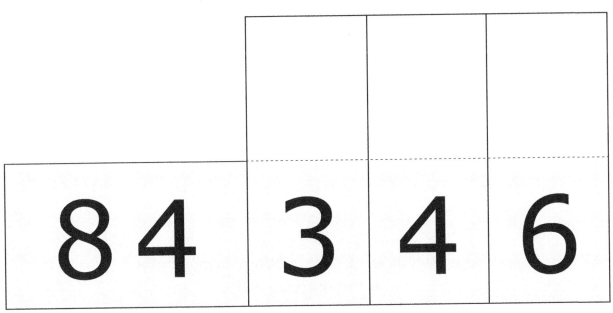

Below are the numbers that you will use to solve the problems. Cut out the numbers on the next page, too. There are some blanks if you need/want more.

This page is left blank for the cutting activity
on the opposite side.

Numbers (continued)

2	2	2	4	4
4	6	6	6	8
8				

This page is left blank for the cutting activity
on the opposite side.

Multiplying Decimals

A. Solve the multiplication problems.

$$
\begin{array}{r}
0.2 \\
\times\ \ 0.8 \\
\hline
\end{array}
\qquad
\begin{array}{r}
0.6 \\
\times\ \ 0.4 \\
\hline
\end{array}
\qquad
\begin{array}{r}
0.5 \\
\times\ \ 0.9 \\
\hline
\end{array}
\qquad
\begin{array}{r}
0.4 \\
\times\ \ 0.2 \\
\hline
\end{array}
$$

$$
\begin{array}{r}
0.05 \\
\times\ \ 3.7 \\
\hline
\end{array}
\qquad
\begin{array}{r}
0.68 \\
\times\ \ 2.4 \\
\hline
\end{array}
\qquad
\begin{array}{r}
0.435 \\
\times\ \ 4.6 \\
\hline
\end{array}
\qquad
\begin{array}{r}
0.957 \\
\times\ \ 0.8 \\
\hline
\end{array}
$$

B. Can you solve this riddle? Use the clues to find the 7-digit number.

Divide 79 by 7. Write the remainder in the tens and thousandths places.

Add the number in the tens place to the number of days in a week. Write the answer in the thousands and ones places.

Multiply the number in the tens place by the number in the ones place and then divide the result by 5. Write the remainder in the hundreds and tenths places.

Add 3 to the number in the tens places. Write the result in the hundredths place.

Date _____

Multiplying Decimals

Solve the multiplication problems.

$$
\begin{array}{r} 0.86 \\ \times\ 0.48 \\ \hline \end{array}
\qquad
\begin{array}{r} 0.96 \\ \times\ 0.59 \\ \hline \end{array}
\qquad
\begin{array}{r} 0.54 \\ \times\ 0.43 \\ \hline \end{array}
\qquad
\begin{array}{r} 0.88 \\ \times\ 0.93 \\ \hline \end{array}
$$

$$
\begin{array}{r} 0.67 \\ \times\ 0.54 \\ \hline \end{array}
\qquad
\begin{array}{r} 0.75 \\ \times\ 0.45 \\ \hline \end{array}
\qquad
\begin{array}{r} 0.62 \\ \times\ 0.12 \\ \hline \end{array}
\qquad
\begin{array}{r} 0.84 \\ \times\ 0.97 \\ \hline \end{array}
$$

$$
\begin{array}{r} 0.61 \\ \times\ 0.95 \\ \hline \end{array}
\qquad
\begin{array}{r} 0.19 \\ \times\ 0.72 \\ \hline \end{array}
\qquad
\begin{array}{r} 0.11 \\ \times\ 0.33 \\ \hline \end{array}
\qquad
\begin{array}{r} 0.31 \\ \times\ 0.84 \\ \hline \end{array}
$$

Date _____

Three Division Formats

Write each division problem in three different formats.

using a division symbol	using a long division symbol	as a fraction
$12 \div 3$ =	=	$^{12}/_3$
=	$6\overline{)57}$	=
=		= $^{17}/_{12}$
=	$25\overline{)48}$	=
$35 \div 35$ =		=
=	$18\overline{)50}$	=
=		= $^{81}/_{95}$
=	$60\overline{)72}$	=
$57 \div 4$ =		=
=	$17\overline{)63}$	=

Date _____

Comparing Fractions and Decimals

Compare the fractions and decimals using < or >. Convert each fraction to a decimal by dividing the numerator by the denominator and then compare the decimals. (Hint: Stop dividing once you find out which number is bigger.)

0.4	$<$	$\frac{1}{2} = 0.5$	0.814	$\bigcirc$	$\frac{5}{7}$
0.85	$\bigcirc$	$\frac{3}{4}$	0.606	$\bigcirc$	$\frac{2}{3}$
0.5	$\bigcirc$	$\frac{2}{5}$	0.042	$\bigcirc$	$\frac{1}{7}$
0.75	$\bigcirc$	$\frac{7}{8}$	0.625	$\bigcirc$	$\frac{5}{9}$
0.45	$\bigcirc$	$\frac{1}{4}$	0.222	$\bigcirc$	$\frac{1}{3}$

YOUR WORK AREA

Date _____

Dividing by 1-Digit & Multiplying Fractions

A. Find the quotient and remainder for each division problem.

$$8\overline{)236} \qquad 7\overline{)150} \qquad 9\overline{)769} \qquad 2\overline{)125}$$

B. Multiply the fractions. Simplify your answers as much as possible.

$$\frac{1}{2} \times \frac{4}{7} = \qquad\qquad \frac{2}{11} \times \frac{1}{6} =$$

$$\frac{3}{4} \times \frac{2}{9} = \qquad\qquad \frac{9}{10} \times \frac{1}{3} =$$

$$\frac{2}{7} \times \frac{4}{6} = \qquad\qquad \frac{7}{12} \times \frac{3}{4} =$$

$$\frac{3}{8} \times \frac{2}{5} = \qquad\qquad \frac{6}{15} \times \frac{5}{9} =$$

Dividing by 1-Digit

Find the quotient and remainder for each division problem.

$8 \overline{)307}$ $\qquad$ $3 \overline{)975}$ $\qquad$ $4 \overline{)898}$ $\qquad$ $7 \overline{)566}$

$5 \overline{)743}$ $\qquad$ $6 \overline{)910}$ $\qquad$ $5 \overline{)132}$ $\qquad$ $2 \overline{)809}$

Date _____

Dividing Fractions

A. Divide the fractions and whole numbers. Simplify your answers if possible.

$2 \div \dfrac{1}{2} =$

$\dfrac{9}{10} \div 3 =$

$\dfrac{2}{3} \div 8 =$

$16 \div \dfrac{8}{9} =$

$\dfrac{1}{2} \div 7 =$

$8 \div \dfrac{4}{10} =$

$9 \div \dfrac{1}{3} =$

$\dfrac{3}{5} \div 12 =$

$\dfrac{3}{5} \div 9 =$

$5 \div \dfrac{7}{10} =$

B. Can you solve this riddle? Use the clues to find the correct fraction.

$\dfrac{7}{8}$	$\dfrac{2}{6}$	$\dfrac{6}{4}$
$\dfrac{3}{12}$	$\dfrac{4}{8}$	$\dfrac{4}{9}$

I am a proper fraction.
My value is bigger than a third.
I am not equivalent to 1/2.
My numerator is even.
What am I? Circle me!

This page is left blank for the cutting activity
on the next page.

Dodecahedron Net

Cut the net out. Fold and paste it together to make a dodecahedron.

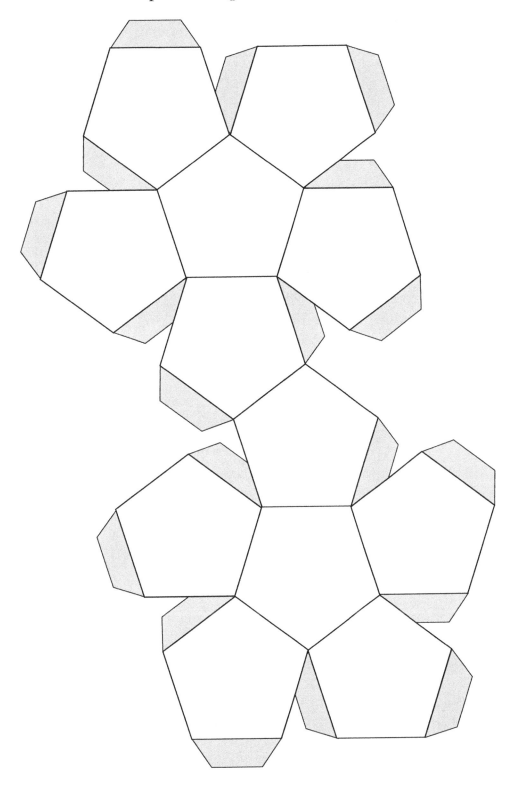

This page is left blank for the cutting activity
on the opposite side.

Date _____

Adding Fractions

Add the fractions with like denominators. Simplify your answer and convert it to a mixed number, if needed.

$$\frac{2}{5} + \frac{2}{5} + \frac{4}{5} =$$

$$\frac{6}{8} + \frac{3}{8} + \frac{5}{8} =$$

$$\frac{3}{9} + \frac{7}{9} + \frac{11}{9} =$$

$$\frac{5}{10} + \frac{4}{10} + \frac{6}{10} =$$

$$\frac{7}{12} + \frac{9}{12} + \frac{4}{12} =$$

$$\frac{6}{15} + \frac{5}{15} + \frac{7}{15} =$$

$$\frac{9}{21} + \frac{13}{21} + \frac{11}{21} =$$

$$\frac{15}{36} + \frac{16}{36} + \frac{17}{36} =$$

Let's Review! I

A. Complete the problems.

$$2635 + \_\_\_\_ = 7350$$

$$5325 - 2647$$

$$\_\_\_\_ \times 5 = 25$$

$$8 \times \_\_\_\_ = 72$$

$$36 \div 6 = \_\_\_\_$$

$$54 \div \_\_\_\_ = 9$$

B. Count by fourths from 5 to 7.

5	$5\frac{1}{4}$							7

C. Solve each word problem. Use the space on the right for your work area.

The store sold 20 cookies for $1.00 each. Their cost per cookie is $0.45. What was the profit?

_____

Three children share a box of candies equally. Each gets 7 candies. There are then 2 candies left. How many candies were in the box originally?

_____

Find the median and range of Kate's math scores:
92, 84, 81, 76, 93, 76, 85

Median: _____   Range: _____

_____

D. Complete the next worksheet, too.

Let's Review! II

D. Write your answers in the blanks provided.

✓ 700 cm = _____ m   ✓ There are _____ nickels in $2.65.

E. How many obtuse angles are within each shape?

_____   _____   _____   _____

F. Find two numbers whose product would be between 250 and 300. Can you find more pairs?

G. James wants to build a rectangular pen with 16 feet of fencing. Assuming the dimensions (length and width) are to be whole numbers, answer the following.

 a) Draw and label all the possible rectangles that James could make.
 b) Find and record the area of each rectangle.
 c) Color in the rectangle that gives the greatest area.

Date _____

Let's Review! I

A. Solve the problems.

$$\begin{array}{r} 57655 \\ + \ 6847 \\ \hline \end{array}$$
$$\begin{array}{r} 71003 \\ - \ 25785 \\ \hline \end{array}$$
$$\begin{array}{r} 100 \\ \times \ 3 \\ \hline \end{array}$$
$$\begin{array}{r} 60 \\ \times \ 8 \\ \hline \end{array}$$
$$\begin{array}{r} 49 \\ \div \ 7 \\ \hline \end{array}$$
$$\begin{array}{r} 32 \\ \div \ 4 \\ \hline \end{array}$$

B. Write your answers in the blanks provided.

✓ What is 300 more than 7,845?   _____

✓ What is the product of 3 and 6?   _____

✓ How many meters are there in 3 kilometers?   _____

✓ It's 2:15 p.m. What time will it be in 45 minutes? _____

✓ What is the digit in the ten thousands place in 23,954? _____

C. Calculate the area (A) of each shape.

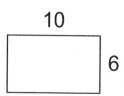

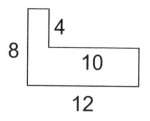

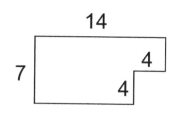

A = _____   A = _____   A = _____

D. Complete the next worksheet, too.

Date _____

Let's Review! II

D. Solve each word problem. Use the space on the right for your work area.

It takes Laura 15 minutes to walk a mile. How long will it take her to walk 6 miles?

_____

Emily runs 20 miles each week. How many weeks will it take her to run 180 miles?

_____

Sam and Matt have $58 in total. Sam has $10 more than Matt. How much money does Matt have?

_____

Matt is studying 2-D shapes. He drew 3 rectangles and then 2 triangles. If he continues this pattern, what shape will he draw as the 28th shape?

_____

E. Can you solve these riddles? Use the clues to find the correct answer.

I have fewer than 25 coins but more than 10 coins. If I put them in piles of 4 or 5, I have 1 coin left over. How many coins do I have?

I have fewer than 40 coins but more than 20 coins. If I put them in piles of 5 or 6, I have 3 coins left over. How many coins do I have?

_____   _____

Date _____

Let's Review! I

A. Complete the problems.

$$
\begin{array}{r}
2485 \\
+\ 6537 \\
\hline
\end{array}
\qquad
\begin{array}{r}
7005 \\
-\ 4738 \\
\hline
\end{array}
\qquad
\begin{array}{r}
11 \\
+16 \\
\hline
50
\end{array}
\qquad
\begin{array}{r}
20 \\
\times\ \ \ \\
\hline
33
\end{array}
\qquad
\begin{array}{r}
55 \\
\div\ \ \ \\
\hline
11
\end{array}
$$

B. Write your answers in the blanks provided.

✓ How many 10s are in 10,000?

_____

✓ How many nickels are in 4 quarters and 7 dimes?

_____

✓ How many lines of symmetry does a square have?

_____

C. Solve each word problem. Use the space on the right for your work area.

A recipe calls for 2 cups of flour to make 8 servings of a cake. How many cups of flour would you need to make 40 servings of cakes?

_____

Mark is making 10 treat bags for his friends. He plans to include a 75¢ orange, a 60¢ apple, and a 25¢ banana. How much money does Mark need?

_____

D. Complete the next worksheet, too.

Let's Review! II

D. Measure each line to the nearest quarter inch.

inches   inches   inches

E. Can you solve these tricky problems? Take your time and think carefully!

How many rectangles can you draw by connecting four dots on the right? Remember that a square is also a type of rectangle!

rectangles

If you multiply me by 113, subtract 93, divide by 8, and then add 241, you get 300. What number am I?

Leah had a workbook of 300 division problems. On the first day she solved 25 problems. On the second day she solved 12 more problems than the first day. If each day she solved 12 more problems than the day before, on what day would she have completed the workbook?

YOUR WORK AREA

Date _____

Let's Review! I

A. Complete the problems.

$$
\begin{array}{r} 8329 \\ + 794 \\ \hline \end{array}
\qquad
\begin{array}{r} 2400 \\ - \\ \hline 1600 \end{array}
\qquad
\begin{array}{r} \\ \times 4 \\ \hline 60 \end{array}
\qquad
\begin{array}{r} 70 \\ \times 8 \\ \hline \end{array}
\qquad
\begin{array}{r} 30 \\ \div \\ \hline 5 \end{array}
\qquad
\begin{array}{r} 36 \\ \div 3 \\ \hline \end{array}
$$

B. Write your answers in the blanks provided.

✓ How many ounces are in half of a pound?

_____

✓ 5 hundreds + 35 tens + 4 tenths + 24 hundredths =

_____

✓ How many pairs of parallel lines does a square have?

_____

C. Write the fraction that represents the shaded part of each rectangle.

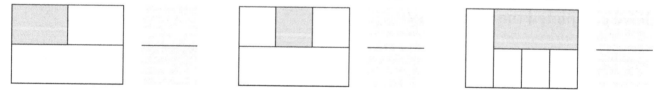

D. Can you solve this geometry puzzle? Take your time and think carefully!

How many squares can you draw by connecting four dots on the right? Remember that a rectangle is not a square! Don't forget to count tilted ones!

_____ squares

E. Complete the next worksheet, too.

Let's Review! II

E. Solve each word problem. Use the space on the right for your work area.

Orson bought 4 cookies. He paid $10 and received $0.32 in change. How much did each cookie cost?

_____

Monica solved 6 worksheets. Each worksheet had 8 problems. Fifteen of the problems were division. How many problems were not division?

_____

Find the median and range of Mia's math scores:

90, 86, 82, 78, 96, 89, 85

Median: Range:
_____

Mia got 92 and 98 this week. Find the new median and range.

Median: Range:
_____

How many years would it take you to spend one million dollars if you spend $500 a month?

_____

How many years would it take you to spend one million dollars if you spend $50 a day?

_____

Answer Key

Lesson 4

Telling Time & Adding 2-Digits

A. Draw the hands on each clock face to show the time.

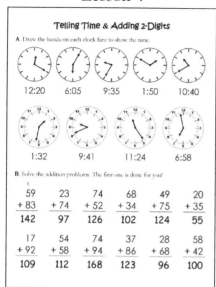

12:20   6:05   9:35   1:50   10:40

1:32   9:41   11:24   6:58

B. Solve the addition problems. The first one is done for you!

59	23	74	68	49	20
+ 83	+ 74	+ 52	+ 34	+ 75	+ 35
142	97	126	102	124	55

17	54	74	37	28	58
+ 92	+ 58	+ 94	+ 86	+ 68	+ 42
109	112	168	123	96	100

Lesson 5

Fractions & Subtracting 2-Digits

A. Write the fraction that represents the shaded parts of each group.

$\frac{2}{3}$ $\frac{1}{4}$

$\frac{2}{4}$ $\frac{2}{5}$

$\frac{3}{4}$ $\frac{3}{5}$

$\frac{1}{3}$ $\frac{4}{7}$

B. Solve the subtraction problems. The first one is done for you!

7 4	72	75	63	29	83
− 58	− 27	− 45	− 49	− 25	− 67
1 6	45	30	14	4	16

84	96	60	95	67	91
− 29	− 56	− 18	− 63	− 30	− 58
55	40	42	32	37	33

Lesson 6

Adding and Subtracting Money

Add or subtract money. Don't forget the currency symbol and decimal point.

$2.00	$5.54	$8.02	$4.65
+ $3.47	+ $0.32	+ $0.16	+ $3.02
$5.47	$5.86	$8.18	$7.67

$4.13	$3.45	$2.46	$4.02
+ $4.76	+ $3.24	+ $6.23	+ $5.57
$8.89	$6.69	$8.69	$9.59

$6.72	$3.42	$2.49	$7.94
+ $2.15	+ $5.36	− $0.32	− $4.52
$8.87	$8.78	$2.17	$3.42

$8.56	$6.48	$2.96	$4.58
− $0.36	− $3.05	− $1.43	− $0.26
$8.20	$3.43	$1.53	$4.32

Pound	Euro	Chinese Yuan	Russian Ruble
£9.58	€8.64	¥9.47	₽7.63
− £3.14	− €3.42	− ¥2.17	− ₽2.20
£6.44	€5.22	¥7.30	₽5.43

Lesson 7

Estimating Sums & Adding 3-Digits

Estimate the sums by rounding the numbers to the nearest hundred. Solve the actual problems for the first four as well.

378 →	400	981 →	1000
+ 239 →	+ 200	+ 863 →	+ 900
617	600	1844	1900

453 →	500	728 →	700
+ 897 →	+ 900	+ 683 →	+ 700
1350	1400	1411	1400

638 →	600	207 →	200
+ 550 →	+ 600	+ 554 →	+ 600
estimate:	1200	estimate:	800

891 →	900	432 →	400
+ 626 →	+ 600	+ 237 →	+ 200
estimate:	1500	estimate:	600

853 →	900	950 →	1000
+ 728 →	+ 700	+ 394 →	+ 400
estimate:	1600	estimate:	1400

Lesson 8

Estimating Differences & Subtracting 3-Digits

Estimate the differences by rounding the numbers to the nearest hundred. Solve the actual problems for the first four as well.

928 →	900	647 →	600
− 529 →	− 500	− 290 →	− 300
399	400	357	300

896 →	900	827 →	800
− 134 →	− 100	− 562 →	− 600
762	800	265	200

761 →	800	743 →	700
− 438 →	− 400	− 286 →	− 300
estimate:	400	estimate:	400

441 →	400	835 →	800
− 373 →	− 400	− 329 →	− 300
estimate:	0	estimate:	500

750 →	800	881 →	900
− 195 →	− 200	− 207 →	− 200
estimate:	600	estimate:	700

Lesson 9

Estimating Sums & Adding 4-Digits

A. Estimate the sums by rounding the numbers to the nearest hundred.

8584 →	8600	9228 →	9200
+ 3205 →	+ 3200	+ 6150 →	+ 6200
11789	11800	15378	15400

3928 →	3900	7868 →	7900
+ 6249 →	+ 6200	+ 4762 →	+ 4800
10177	10100	12630	12700

B. Estimate the sums by rounding the numbers to the nearest thousand.

4352 →	4000	8334 →	8000
+ 6787 →	+ 7000	+ 5607 →	+ 6000
11139	11000	13941	14000

2983 →	3000	7500 →	8000
+ 6065 →	+ 6000	+ 7456 →	+ 7000
9048	9000	14956	15000

C. Choose four problems above to find the exact sums. You can solve all eight problems if you want!

Lesson 10

Estimating Differences & Subtracting 4-Digits

A. Estimate the differences by rounding the numbers to the nearest hundred.

4665 →	4700	8578 →	8600
− 1258 →	− 1300	− 4937 →	− 4900
3407	3400	3641	3700

5930 →	5900	7278 →	7300
− 1675 →	− 1700	− 3693 →	− 3700
4255	4200	3585	3600

B. Estimate the differences by rounding the numbers to the nearest thousand.

8362 →	8000	7432 →	7000
− 5756 →	− 6000	− 5867 →	− 6000
2606	2000	1565	1000

9116 →	9000	5819 →	6000
− 6569 →	− 7000	− 2982 →	− 3000
2547	2000	2837	3000

C. Choose four problems above to find the exact differences. You can solve all eight problems if you want!

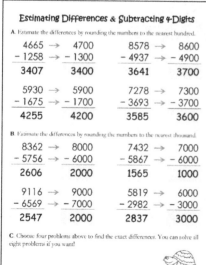

Lesson 13

Place Value and Expanded Notation

A. How many hundreds, tens, and ones are in the number 405?

405 = 4 hundreds + 0 tens + 5 ones

B. Write the number 405 in expanded form, or expanded notation.

405 = 400 + 5

C. Write each number in standard form.

70 + 6 = 76	800 + 20 + 9 = 829
500 + 4 = 504	2,000 + 70 + 1 = 2,071
200 + 50 = 250	3,000 + 100 + 7 = 3,107
900 + 40 = 940	8,000 + 200 + 90 + 5 = 8,295

D. Write each number in expanded form.

82 =	80 + 2
463 =	400 + 60 + 3
305 =	300 + 5
350 =	300 + 50
5,281 =	5,000 + 200 + 80 + 1

Lesson 18

Place Value to Millions

Write the value of each underlined digit in words.

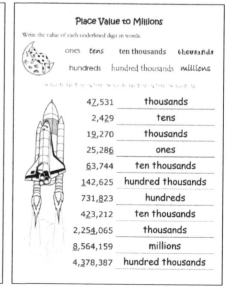

ones   tens   ten thousands   thousands
hundreds   hundred thousands   millions

4<u>7</u>,531	thousands
2,4<u>2</u>9	tens
1<u>9</u>,270	thousands
25,28<u>6</u>	ones
<u>6</u>3,744	ten thousands
1<u>4</u>2,625	hundred thousands
731,<u>8</u>23	hundreds
4<u>2</u>3,212	ten thousands
2,2<u>5</u>4,065	thousands
<u>8</u>,564,159	millions
4,<u>3</u>78,387	hundred thousands

Lesson 19

Place Value to Millions

A. Write each number in expanded form.

32,917 =	30,000 + 2,000 + 900 + 10 + 7
54,890 =	50,000 + 4,000 + 800 + 90
672,039 =	600,000 + 70,000 + 2,000 + 30 + 9
2,803,426 =	2,000,000 + 800,000 + 3,000 + 400 + 20 + 6
4,367,204 =	4,000,000 + 300,000 + 60,000 + 7,000 + 200 + 4

B. Write 4-digit numbers. Then write each number in expanded form.

_____ = _____

_____ = _____

C. Write 5-digit numbers. Then write each number in expanded form.

_____ = _____

_____ = _____

Lesson 20

Place Value to Millions

A. Write each number in standard or expanded form to complete the table.

7,325	7,000 + 300 + 20 + 5
406,932	400,000 + 6,000 + 900 + 30 + 2
9,312,507	9,000,000 + 300,000 + 10,000 + 2,000 + 500 + 7

B. Write each number in standard or word form to complete the table.

12,368	twelve thousand, three hundred sixty-eight
242,719	two hundred forty-two thousand, seven hundred nineteen
4,502,587	four million, five hundred two thousand, five hundred eighty-seven

Lesson 25

Mental Math Strategies

A. Add or subtract mentally. Use expanded notation or rounding.

58 + 66 = __124__	85 − 43 = __42__
372 + 798 = __1170__	525 − 456 = __69__
852 + 247 = __1099__	787 + 434 = __1221__

B. Solve each word problem mentally.

Ron collects stamps. He collected 58 flower stamps and 46 bird stamps. How many stamps did Ron collect all together?

__104 stamps__

Roger has 966 red marbles and 759 blue marbles. Mark has 834 red marbles and 763 blue marbles. Who has more marbles?

__Roger__

Grace had 987 smiley stickers. She gave 879 of them to her sister Angela. How many stickers does Grace have now?

__108 stickers__

Mia needs to solve 35 problems. She has solved 18 problems so far. How many problems does Mia still need to solve?

__17 problems__

Sam read 176 pages of his reading assignment last week. He read 189 pages this week. How many pages did Sam read in all?

__365 pages__

The candy store sold 453 candies last week. It sold 328 candies this week. How many candies did the candy store sell in total?

__781 candies__

Lesson 26

Multiplying 2-Digits

Let's practice multiplying bigger numbers. The first two are done for you!

16 × 4 = 64	98 × 4 = 392	41 × 3 = 123	41 × 30 = 1230	27 × 5 = 135
81 × 6 = 486	27 × 3 = 81	39 × 2 = 78	68 × 5 = 340	50 × 4 = 200
52 × 4 = 208	36 × 7 = 252	96 × 8 = 768	23 × 2 = 46	34 × 9 = 306

Lesson 28

Multiplying 2-Digits

Solve the multiplication problems.

75 × 57 = 4275	35 × 49 = 1715	42 × 68 = 2856	79 × 60 = 4740	95 × 84 = 7980
52 × 26 = 1352	88 × 37 = 3256	39 × 46 = 1794	63 × 35 = 2205	80 × 43 = 3440
10 × 72 = 720	48 × 53 = 2544	26 × 65 = 1690	29 × 75 = 2175	86 × 23 = 1978

Lesson 29

Multiplying 2-Digits

Solve the multiplication problems.

43 × 86 = 3698	90 × 57 = 5130	75 × 36 = 2700	25 × 73 = 1825	63 × 48 = 3024
28 × 65 = 1820	56 × 47 = 2632	19 × 82 = 1558	93 × 68 = 6324	79 × 30 = 2370
85 × 17 = 1445	50 × 72 = 3600	43 × 86 = 3698	92 × 55 = 5060	64 × 29 = 1856

Lesson 36

Multiplying 3-Digits

Solve the multiplication problems. Two problems are done for you!

875 × 6 = 5,250	616 × 4 = 2,464	411 × 56 = 23,016	251 × 98 = 24,598
746 × 58 = 43,268	362 × 68 = 24,616	147 × 95 = 13,965	950 × 27 = 25,650
906 × 43 = 38,958	578 × 34 = 19,652	482 × 91 = 43,862	326 × 27 = 8,802

Lesson 38

Multiplying 3-Digits

Solve the multiplication problems.

720 × 532 = 383,040	495 × 253 = 125,235	787 × 321 = 252,627	538 × 694 = 373,372
578 × 975 = 563,550	810 × 641 = 519,210	452 × 930 = 420,360	293 × 382 = 111,926

Lesson 39

Multiplying 3-Digits

Solve the multiplication problems.

201 × 374 = 75,174	392 × 549 = 215,208	800 × 270 = 216,000	476 × 305 = 145,180
391 × 367 = 143,497	125 × 746 = 93,250	820 × 342 = 280,440	564 × 486 = 274,104

Lesson 41

Multiplying 2-Digits

Solve the multiplication problems.

31 × 7 = 217	46 × 8 = 368	34 × 9 = 306	57 × 5 = 285	48 × 0 = 0
50 × 8 = 400	84 × 2 = 168	17 × 1 = 17	95 × 6 = 570	63 × 7 = 441
61 × 9 = 549	39 × 7 = 273	58 × 3 = 174	82 × 4 = 328	71 × 3 = 213

Lesson 42

Multiplying 2-Digits

Solve the multiplication problems.

20 × 42 = 840	15 × 38 = 570	54 × 41 = 2214	63 × 25 = 1575	23 × 94 = 2162
34 × 22 = 748	95 × 85 = 8075	48 × 73 = 3504	21 × 60 = 1260	86 × 36 = 3096
50 × 92 = 4600	16 × 73 = 1168	62 × 49 = 3038	39 × 52 = 2028	87 × 29 = 2523

Lesson 43

Multiplying 3-Digits

Solve the multiplication problems.

511 × 73 = 37,303	830 × 19 = 15,770	489 × 65 = 31,785	574 × 61 = 35,014
604 × 28 = 16,912	427 × 67 = 28,609	509 × 52 = 26,468	781 × 90 = 70,290
895 × 81 = 72,495	248 × 43 = 10,664	758 × 66 = 50,028	677 × 29 = 19,633

Lesson 44

Multiplying 3-Digits

Solve the multiplication problems.

908 × 122 = 110,776	786 × 195 = 153,270	357 × 774 = 276,318	569 × 665 = 378,385
914 × 558 = 510,012	306 × 392 = 119,952	832 × 747 = 621,504	138 × 376 = 51,888
316 × 806 = 254,696	643 × 311 = 199,973	419 × 570 = 238,830	845 × 432 = 365,040

Lesson 45

Estimating Products

A. Estimate each product by rounding the top number to the nearest hundred and the bottom number to the nearest ten and then multiplying the first digits.

458 → 500 × 34 → × 30 estimate: 15,000	325 → 300 × 49 → × 50 estimate: 15,000
913 → 900 × 54 → × 50 estimate: 45,000	769 → 800 × 86 → × 90 estimate: 72,000
521 → 500 × 87 → × 90 estimate: 45,000	850 → 900 × 93 → × 90 estimate: 81,000
926 → 900 × 11 → × 10 estimate: 9,000	392 → 400 × 35 → × 40 estimate: 16,000

B. Estimate the product by rounding the first number to the nearest thousand and the second number to the nearest hundred.

$5{,}678 \times 504 = 6000 \times 500 = 3{,}000{,}000$

Lesson 46

Estimating Products

A. Estimate each product by rounding the top number to the nearest hundred and the bottom number to the nearest ten and then multiplying the first digits. Solve the actual problems as well.

433 → 400 × 38 → × 40 16,454 16,000	321 → 300 × 14 → × 10 4,494 3,000
797 → 800 × 53 → × 50 42,241 40,000	704 → 700 × 62 → × 60 43,648 42,000

B. Find the difference between the actual and the estimated answers.

16,454 −16,000 454	4,494 − 3,000 1,494	42,241 −40,000 2,241	43,648 −42,000 1,648

Lesson 54

Fraction Word Problems

For each word problem, make a labeled sketch and write an equation. Explain your answer to someone. The first one is done for you!

After school, Adam spent $\frac{1}{4}$ of an hour on math, $\frac{1}{4}$ on reading, and $\frac{1}{4}$ on science. What fraction of an hour did he spend on studying?

Labeled Sketch:

¼	¼	¼
math	reading	science

Equation:

$$\frac{1}{4} + \frac{1}{4} + \frac{1}{4} = \frac{3}{4}$$

Kyle had $\frac{5}{6}$ of a carton of eggs. After he used some to bake cookies, $\frac{1}{6}$ of the carton was left. What fraction of the carton did Kyle use?

Labeled Sketch:

⅙	⅙	⅙	⅙	⅙
Left				Used

Equation:

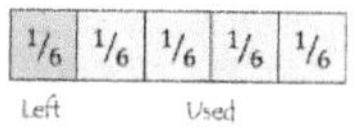

$$\frac{5}{6} - \frac{1}{6} = \frac{4}{6}$$

The morning break lasts $\frac{5}{8}$ of an hour. Danny spent $\frac{2}{8}$ of an hour jumping rope. What fraction of an hour did he have left after that?

Labeled Sketch:

⅛	⅛	⅛	⅛	⅛
Left				Spent

Equation:

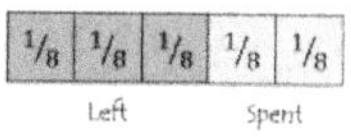

$$\frac{5}{8} - \frac{2}{8} = \frac{3}{8}$$

Lesson 58

Fraction Word Problems

For each word problem, make a labeled sketch and write an equation. Explain your answer to someone. The first one is done for you!

The store had $\frac{5}{6}$ of a box of apples. It sold $\frac{3}{6}$ of the box in the morning. What fraction of the box did the store have left after that?

Labeled Sketch:

Equation:

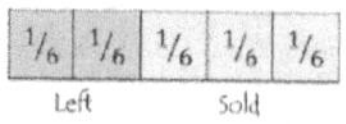

$$\frac{5}{6} - \frac{3}{6} = \frac{2}{6}$$

Walter bought three boxes of fruit. They weigh $1\frac{2}{6}$ pounds, $1\frac{2}{6}$ pounds, and $2\frac{1}{6}$ pounds. What is the total weight of the three boxes?

Labeled Sketch:

Equation:

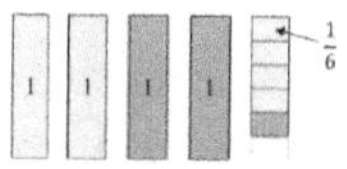

$$1\frac{2}{6} + 1\frac{2}{6} + 2\frac{1}{6} = 4\frac{5}{6}$$

Tracy used $1\frac{2}{8}$ gallons of red paint, $2\frac{1}{8}$ gallons of blue paint, and $2\frac{3}{8}$ gallons of white paint to paint her house. How many gallons of paint did Tracy use in total?

Labeled Sketch:

Equation:

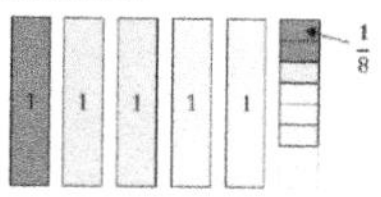

$$1\frac{2}{8} + 2\frac{1}{8} + 2\frac{3}{8} = 5\frac{6}{8}$$

Lesson 59

Fraction Word Problems

For each word problem, make a labeled sketch and write an equation. Explain your answer to someone. The first one is done for you!

The city has a beautiful 2 mile trail. Claire walked the first $1\frac{1}{4}$ miles of the trail and ran the rest. How far did she run?

Labeled Sketch:

Equation:

$$2 - 1\frac{1}{4} = \frac{3}{4}$$

Matt went for a walk on the trail. He walked $\frac{3}{4}$ of a mile. Then he turned around and walked back to the start of the trail. How many miles did he walk in all?

Labeled Sketch:

Equation:

$$\frac{3}{4} + \frac{3}{4} = \frac{6}{4} = 1\frac{2}{4}$$

Jacob decided to run the whole trail. After running $1\frac{3}{8}$ miles, he got tired and decided to walk the rest. How far did he have to walk to finish the trail?

Labeled Sketch:

Equation:

$$2 - 1\frac{3}{8} = \frac{5}{8}$$

Lesson 60

Fraction Word Problems

For each word problem, make a labeled sketch and write an equation. Explain your answer to someone. The track is 2 miles long.

Chris went for a walk on the trail. He walked $1\frac{1}{8}$ of a mile. Then he turned around and walked back to the start. How many miles did he walk in all?

Labeled Sketch:

Equation:

$1\frac{1}{8} + 1\frac{1}{8} = 2\frac{2}{8}$

Laura ran to the $\frac{3}{4}$ mile marker and ran back to the $\frac{1}{4}$ mile marker. Then she turned around and ran the rest of the trail. How many miles did she run in all?

Labeled Sketch:

Equation:

$\frac{3}{4} + \frac{2}{4} + 1\frac{3}{4} = 3$

Everyday Justin walks the trail. When he gets to the $1\frac{1}{2}$ mile marker, he turns around and walks back to the start. How many miles does he walk in 5 days?

Labeled Sketch:

Start   ½   1   1½   2 miles

per day

Equation:

$2\frac{2}{4} + 2\frac{2}{4} + 2\frac{2}{4} + 2\frac{2}{4} + 2\frac{2}{4} = 12\frac{2}{4}$

Lesson 79

Multiplying Decimals

A. Solve the multiplication problems.

0.2	0.6	0.5	0.4
x 0.8	x 0.4	x 0.9	x 0.2
0.16	0.24	0.45	0.08

0.05	0.68	0.435	0.957
x 3.7	x 2.4	x 4.6	x 0.8
0.185	1.632	2.001	0.7656

B. Can you solve this riddle? Use the clues to find the 7-digit number.

9	,	3	2	9	.	3	5	2

Divide 79 by 7. Write the remainder in the tens and thousandths places.

Add the number in the tens place to the number of days in a week. Write the answer in the thousands and ones places.

Multiply the number in the tens place by the number in the ones place and then divide the result by 5. Write the remainder in the hundreds and tenths places.

Add 3 to the number in the tens places. Write the result in the hundredths place.

Lesson 80

Multiplying Decimals

Solve the multiplication problems.

0.86	0.96	0.54	0.88
x 0.48	x 0.59	x 0.43	x 0.93
0.4128	0.5664	0.2322	0.8184

0.67	0.75	0.62	0.84
x 0.54	x 0.45	x 0.12	x 0.97
0.3618	0.3375	0.0744	0.8148

0.61	0.19	0.11	0.31
x 0.95	x 0.72	x 0.33	x 0.84
0.5795	0.1368	0.0363	0.2604

Lesson 85

Three Division Formats

Write each division problem in three different formats.

using a division symbol		using a long division symbol		as a fraction
$12 \div 3$	=	$3\overline{)12}$	=	$^{12}/_{3}$
$57 \div 6$	=	$6\overline{)57}$	=	$^{57}/_{6}$
$17 \div 12$	=	$12\overline{)17}$	=	$^{17}/_{12}$
$48 \div 25$	=	$25\overline{)48}$	=	$^{48}/_{25}$
$35 \div 35$	=	$35\overline{)35}$	=	$^{35}/_{35}$
$50 \div 18$	=	$18\overline{)50}$	=	$^{50}/_{18}$
$81 \div 95$	=	$95\overline{)81}$	=	$^{81}/_{95}$
$72 \div 60$	=	$60\overline{)72}$	=	$^{72}/_{60}$
$57 \div 4$	=	$4\overline{)57}$	=	$^{57}/_{4}$
$63 \div 17$	=	$17\overline{)63}$	=	$^{63}/_{17}$

Lesson 86

Comparing Fractions and Decimals

Compare the fractions and decimals using < or >. Convert each fraction to a decimal by dividing the numerator by the denominator and then compare the decimals. (Hint: Stop dividing once you find out which number is bigger.)

$0.4 \; (<) \; \frac{1}{2} = 0.5$ $0.814 \; (>) \; \frac{5}{7} = 0.71...$

$0.85 \; (>) \; \frac{3}{4} = 0.75$ $0.606 \; (<) \; \frac{2}{3} = 0.66...$

$0.5 \; (>) \; \frac{2}{5} = 0.4$ $0.042 \; (<) \; \frac{1}{7} = 0.14...$

$0.75 \; (<) \; \frac{7}{8} = 0.875$ $0.625 \; (>) \; \frac{5}{9} = 0.55...$

$0.45 \; (>) \; \frac{1}{4} = 0.25$ $0.222 \; (<) \; \frac{1}{3} = 0.33...$

YOUR WORK AREA

Lesson 92

Dividing by 1-Digit & Multiplying Fractions

A. Find the quotient and remainder for each division problem.

29 R4 $8\overline{)236}$ 21 R3 $7\overline{)150}$ 85 R4 $9\overline{)769}$ 62 R1 $2\overline{)125}$

B. Multiply the fractions. Simplify your answers as much as possible.

$\frac{1}{2} \times \frac{4}{7} = \frac{4}{14} = \frac{2}{7}$ $\frac{2}{11} \times \frac{1}{6} = \frac{2}{66} = \frac{1}{33}$

$\frac{3}{4} \times \frac{2}{9} = \frac{6}{36} = \frac{1}{6}$ $\frac{9}{10} \times \frac{1}{3} = \frac{9}{30} = \frac{3}{10}$

$\frac{2}{7} \times \frac{4}{6} = \frac{8}{42} = \frac{4}{21}$ $\frac{7}{12} \times \frac{3}{4} = \frac{21}{48} = \frac{7}{16}$

$\frac{3}{8} \times \frac{2}{5} = \frac{6}{40} = \frac{3}{20}$ $\frac{6}{15} \times \frac{5}{9} = \frac{30}{135} = \frac{2}{9}$

Lesson 94

Dividing by 1-Digit

Find the quotient and remainder for each division problem.

38 R3 $8\overline{)307}$ 325 $3\overline{)975}$ 224 R2 $4\overline{)898}$ 80 R6 $7\overline{)566}$

148 R3 $5\overline{)743}$ 151 R4 $6\overline{)910}$ 26 R2 $5\overline{)132}$ 404 R1 $2\overline{)809}$

Lesson 95

Dividing Fractions

A. Divide the fractions and whole numbers. Simplify your answers if possible.

$2 \div \frac{1}{2} = 4$ $\frac{9}{10} \div 3 = \frac{9}{30} = \frac{3}{10}$

$\frac{2}{3} \div 8 = \frac{2}{24} = \frac{1}{12}$ $16 \div \frac{8}{9} = \frac{144}{8} = 18$

$\frac{1}{2} \div 7 = \frac{1}{14}$ $8 \div \frac{4}{10} = \frac{80}{4} = 20$

$9 \div \frac{1}{3} = 27$ $\frac{3}{5} \div 12 = \frac{3}{60} = \frac{1}{20}$

$\frac{3}{5} \div 9 = \frac{3}{45} = \frac{1}{15}$ $5 \div \frac{7}{10} = \frac{50}{7} = 7\frac{1}{7}$

B. Can you solve this riddle? Use the clues to find the correct fraction.

$\frac{7}{8}$	$\frac{2}{6}$	$\frac{6}{4}$
$\frac{3}{12}$	$\frac{4}{8}$	$\frac{4}{9}$

I am a proper fraction.
My value is bigger than a third.
I am not equivalent to 1/2.
My numerator is even.
What am I? Circle me!

Lesson 141

Adding Fractions

Add the fractions with like denominators. Simplify your answer and convert it to a mixed number, if needed.

$\frac{2}{5} + \frac{1}{5} + \frac{5}{5} = \frac{8}{5} = 1\frac{3}{5}$

$\frac{6}{8} + \frac{3}{8} + \frac{5}{8} = \frac{14}{8} = \frac{7}{4} = 1\frac{3}{4}$

$\frac{3}{9} + \frac{7}{9} + \frac{11}{9} = \frac{21}{9} = \frac{7}{3} = 2\frac{1}{3}$

$\frac{5}{10} + \frac{4}{10} + \frac{6}{10} = \frac{15}{10} = \frac{3}{2} = 1\frac{1}{2}$

$\frac{7}{12} + \frac{9}{12} + \frac{4}{12} = \frac{20}{12} = \frac{5}{3} = 1\frac{2}{3}$

$\frac{6}{15} + \frac{5}{15} + \frac{7}{15} = \frac{18}{15} = \frac{6}{5} = 1\frac{1}{5}$

$\frac{9}{21} + \frac{13}{21} + \frac{11}{21} = \frac{33}{21} = \frac{11}{7} = 1\frac{4}{7}$

$\frac{15}{36} + \frac{16}{36} + \frac{17}{36} = \frac{48}{36} = \frac{4}{3} = 1\frac{1}{3}$

Lesson 151

Let's Review! I

A. Complete the problems.

2635	5325	5	8	36	54
+ 4715	− 2647	x 5	x 9	÷ 6	÷ 6
7350	2678	25	72	6	9

B. Count by fourths from 5 to 7.

5   $5\frac{1}{4}$ $5\frac{1}{2}$ $5\frac{3}{4}$ 6 $6\frac{1}{4}$ $6\frac{1}{2}$ $6\frac{3}{4}$ 7

C. Solve each word problem. Use the space on the right for your work area.

The store sold 20 cookies for $1.00 each. Their cost per cookie is $0.45. What was the profit?

$11.00

Three children share a box of candies equally. Each gets 7 candies. There are then 2 candies left. How many candies were in the box originally?

23 candies

Find the median and range of Kate's math scores:
92, 84, 81, 76, 93, 76, 85

Median: 84   Range: 17

D. Complete the next worksheet, too.

Lesson 151

Let's Review! II

D. Write your answers in the blanks provided.

✓ 700 cm = 7 m   ✓ There are 53 nickels in $2.65.

E. How many obtuse angles are within each shape?

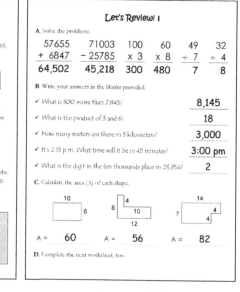

0   2   6   1

F. Find two numbers whose product would be between 250 and 300. Can you find more pairs?

2 x 130 = 260   15 x 18 = 270
3 x 95 = 285   12 x 24 = 288

G. James wants to build a rectangular pen with 16 feet of fencing. Assuming the dimensions (length and width) are to be whole numbers, answer the following:
a) Draw and label all the possible rectangles that James could make.
b) Find and record the area of each rectangle.
c) Color in the rectangle that gives the greatest area.

L = 1	L = 2	L = 3	L = 4
W = 7	W = 6	W = 5	W = 4
A = 7	A = 12	A = 15	A = 16

Lesson 152

Let's Review! I

A. Solve the problems.

57655	71003	100	60	49	32
+ 6847	− 25785	x 3	x 8	÷ 7	÷ 4
64,502	45,218	300	480	7	8

B. Write your answers in the blanks provided.

✓ What is 300 more than 7,845? 8,145
✓ Find the product of 3 and 6? 18
✓ How many meters are there in 3 kilometers? 3,000
✓ It's 2:15 p.m. What time will it be in 45 minutes? 3:00 pm
✓ What is the digit in the ten thousands place in 25,954? 2

C. Calculate the area (A) of each shape.

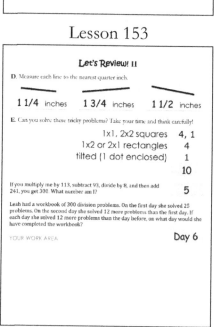

A = 60   A = 56   A = 82

D. Complete the next worksheet, too.

Lesson 152

Let's Review! II

D. Solve each word problem. Use the space on the right for your work area.

It takes Laura 15 minutes to walk a mile. How long will it take her to walk 6 miles?

90 minutes

Emily runs 20 miles each week. How many weeks will it take her to run 180 miles?

9 weeks

Sam and Matt have $58 in total. Sam has $10 more than Matt. How much money does Matt have?

$24

Matt is studying 2-D shapes. He drew 3 rectangles and then 2 triangles. If he continues this pattern, what shape will he draw as the 28th shape?

Rectangle

E. Can you solve these riddles? Use the clues to find the correct answer.

I have fewer than 25 coins but more than 10 coins. If I put them in piles of 4 or 5, I have 1 coin left over. How many coins do I have?

21 coins

I have fewer than 40 coins but more than 20 coins. If I put them in piles of 5 or 6, I have 3 coins left over. How many coins do I have?

33 coins

Lesson 153

Let's Review! I

A. Complete the problems.

2485	7005	34	11	20	55
+ 6537	− 4738	+16	x 3	x 7	÷ 5
9,022	2,267	50	33	140	11

B. Write your answers in the blanks provided.

✓ How many 10s are in 10,000? 1,000
✓ How many nickels are in 4 quarters and 7 dimes? 34
✓ How many lines of symmetry does a square have? 4

C. Solve each word problem. Use the space on the right for your work area.

A recipe calls for 2 cups of flour to make 8 servings of a cake. How many cups of flour would you need to make 40 servings of cakes?

10 cups

Mark is making 10 treat bags for his friends. He plans to include a 75¢ orange, a 60¢ apple, and a 25¢ banana. How much money does Mark need?

$16

D. Complete the next worksheet, too.

Lesson 153

Let's Review! II

D. Measure each line to the nearest quarter inch.

1 1/4 inches   1 3/4 inches   1 1/2 inches

E. Can you solve these tricky problems? Take your time and think carefully!

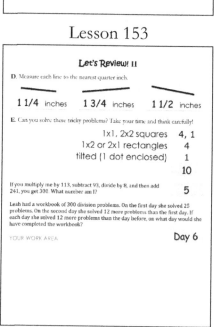

1x1, 2x2 squares 4, 1
1x2 or 2x1 rectangles 4
tilted (1 dot enclosed) 1
10

If you multiply me by 113, subtract 93, divide by 8, and then add 241, you get 300. What number am I? 5

Leah had a workbook of 300 division problems. On the first day she solved 25 problems. On the second day she solved 12 more problems than the first day. If each day she solved 12 more problems than the day before, on what day would she have completed the workbook?

YOUR WORK AREA   Day 6

Lesson 154

Let's Review! I

A. Complete the problems.

8329	2400	15	70	30	36
+ 794	− 800	x 4	x 8	÷ 6	÷ 3
9123	1600	60	560	5	12

B. Write your answers in the blanks provided.

✓ How many ounces are in half of a pound? 8 oz
✓ 5 hundreds + 55 tens + 4 tenths + 24 hundredths = 850.64
✓ How many pairs of parallel lines does a square have? 2 pairs

C. Write the fraction that represents the shaded part of each rectangle.

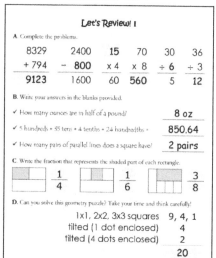

$\frac{1}{4}$ $\frac{1}{6}$ $\frac{3}{8}$

D. Can you solve this geometry puzzle? Take your time and think carefully!

1x1, 2x2, 3x3 squares 9, 4, 1
tilted (1 dot enclosed) 4
tilted (4 dots enclosed) 2
20

E. Complete the next worksheet, too.

Lesson 154

Let's Review! II

E. Solve each word problem. Use the space on the right for your work area.

Orson bought 4 cookies. He paid $10 and received $0.32 in change. How much did each cookie cost?

$2.42

Monica solved 6 worksheets. Each worksheet had 8 problems. Fifteen of the problems were division. How many problems were not division?

33 problems

Find the median and range of Mia's math scores:
90, 86, 82, 78, 96, 89, 85

Median: 86   Range: 18

Mia got 92 and 98 this week. Find the new median and range.

Median: 89   Range: 20

How many years would it take you to spend one million dollars if you spend $500 a month?

167 years

How many years would it take you to spend one million dollars if you spend $50 a day?

55 years

Made in the USA
Monee, IL
28 August 2021